MINIFIGURE MAYHEM

by Beth Davies and Helen Murray

This LEGO® book belongs to:

KT-155-483

Penguin
Random
House

Editors Beth Davies and Helen Murray
Designers Sam Bartlett and Jenny Edwards
Pre-production Producer Marc Staples
Senior Producer Lloyd Robertson
Managing Editor Paula Regan
Managing Art Editor Jo Connor
Publisher Julie Ferris
Art Director Lisa Lanzarini
Publishing Director Simon Beecroft

DK would like to thank Kirsten Grant and
Emma Pritchard from the World Book Day team.

First published in Great Britain in 2019 by
Dorling Kindersley Limited
80 Strand, London WC2R 0RL
A Penguin Random House Company

10 9 8 7 6 5 4 3 2 1
001-313505-Feb/2019

Page design © 2019 Dorling
Kindersley Limited
DK, a Division of Penguin Random
House LLC

A CIP catalogue record for this book
is available from the British Library.

ISBN: 978-0-24137-073-5

Printed in China

A WORLD OF IDEAS:
SEE ALL THERE IS TO KNOW

www.dk.com
www.LEGO.com

CELEBRATE STORIES. LOVE READING.

This book has been specially written and published to celebrate **World Book Day**.
We are a charity who offers every child and young person the opportunity to read and
love books by giving you the chance to have a book of your own. To find out more,
and for oodles of fun activities and reading recommendations to continue your reading
journey, visit **worldbookday.com**

World Book Day in the UK and Ireland is made possible by generous sponsorship from
National Book Tokens, booksellers, participating publishers, authors and illustrators.
The £1* book tokens are a gift from your local bookseller.

*World Book Day works in partnership with a number of charities, all of whom are working
to encourage a love of reading for pleasure.*

The National Literacy Trust is an independent charity that encourages children and young
people to enjoy reading. Just 10 minutes of reading every day can make a big difference to
how well you do at school and to how successful you could be in life. **literacytrust.org.uk**

The Reading Agency inspires people of all ages and backgrounds to read for pleasure and
empowerment. They run the Summer Reading Challenge in partnership with libraries; they also
support reading groups in schools and libraries all year round. Find out more and join your
local library. **summerreadingchallenge.org.uk**

World Book Day also facilitates fundraising for:
Book Aid International, an international book donation and library development charity.
Every year, they provide one million books to libraries and schools in communities where
children would otherwise have little or no opportunity to read. **bookaid.org**

Read for Good, who motivate children in schools to read for fun through its sponsored
read, which thousands of schools run on World Book Day and throughout the year.
The money raised provides new books and resident storytellers in all the children's
hospitals in the UK. **readforgood.org**

*€1.50 in Ireland

Contents

OUT OF THIS WORLD

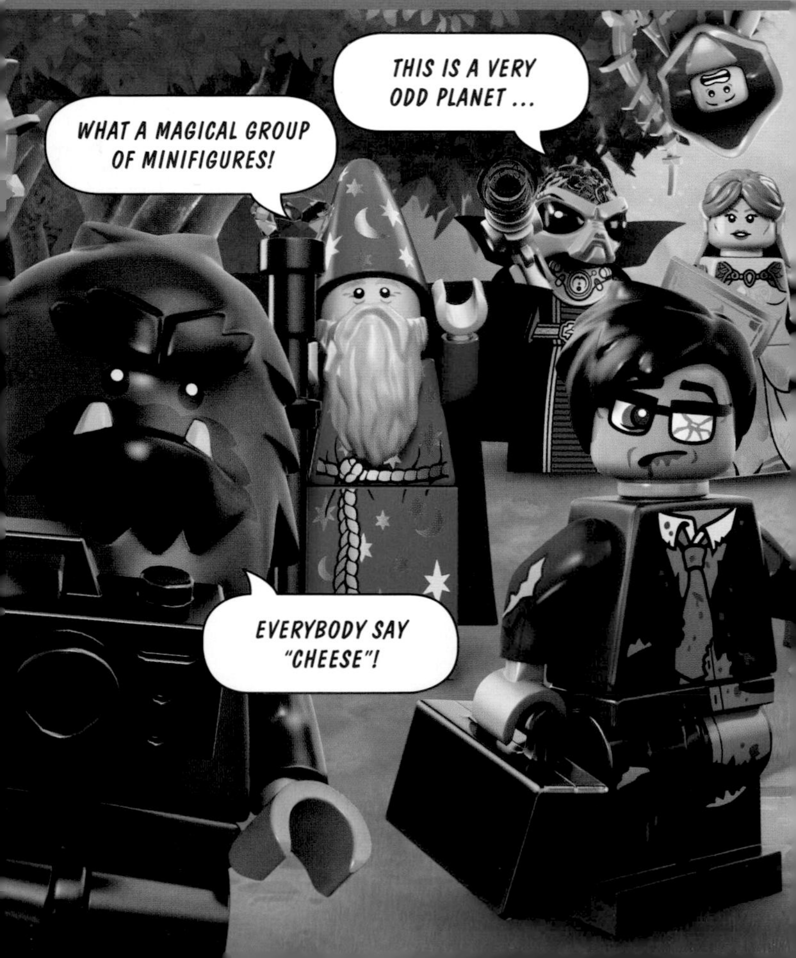

Aliens, monsters and other magical minifigures live happily together.

I SAY ... F-L-Y!
YOU SAY ... FLY-FLY-FLY!

ZOMBIE TIMES
BRAAAINS!

IS THAT A NEW POTION, PROFESSOR?

YES. BUT IT HAS SOME UNUSUAL SIDE EFFECTS!

Mini Facts

Likes Stripy socks

Dislikes Getting broom-sick

Favourite animals Bats and cats

Wacky Witch

Life is no fairy tale for the unlucky Wacky Witch! Her grumpy cat is too busy napping to help the Witch with her spells, and bugs keep eating her gingerbread house!

> WHAT IS A WIZARD'S FAVOURITE SCHOOL LESSON?
>
> SPELLING!

Muddled magician

The wise old wizard has read every magic book in the land and has a potion to solve every problem. If only he could remember where he left them all ...

Zombie Businessman

Everything this Zombie does is slow! He struggles to get up when his alarm clock rings. He walks to work slowly. His coffee is always cold because it takes him so long to start drinking it!

> WHAT DO YOU CALL A SLEEPY MONSTER?
>
> A ZZZZZZZOMBIE.

Full of cheer

Unlike the Zombie Businessman, the Zombie Cheerleader has plenty of energy. She shows up to support her school sports teams at every game. Go Zombies!

Mini Facts

Likes Weekends

Dislikes Urgent deadlines

Favourite newspaper Zombie Times

Mini Facts

Likes Helping those in need

Dislikes Evil villains

Sidekick An enchanted singing sword

Elf Maiden

The Elf Maiden does not want to stay hidden in the Elflands. She is on a quest to find adventure! This brave hero journeys around the land armed with her golden sword and shield. Her pointed ears never miss a cry for help.

WHAT IS THE FIRST THING ELVES LEARN IN SCHOOL?

THE ELF-ABET!

Friendly face
The Faun fills his forest home with music. His favourite instrument is a flute. This odd creature has the body of a man, but the legs and horns of a goat.

Square Foot

Who is the mysterious Square Foot? People say he is a huge, hairy monster, but all they can ever find is his big, square footprints. This gentle giant really just wants some peace and quiet to practise his photography.

HOW DO SNAKES SIGN THEIR LETTERS?

WITH LOVE AND HISSES!

Ssshh, sssnakes!

Unlike Square Foot, Medusa finds it very hard to stay silent. She tries to sneak up on people and turn them into stone, but her hair is made of loud hissing snakes!

Mini Facts

Likes Nature and wildlife

Dislikes Buying shoes

Favourite accessory Digital camera

CHALLENGE!

Stack a minifigure

See how many minifigures you can stack before they tip over! Try stacking against the clock or challenge a friend.

I HOPE MY FLIPPERS DON'T FALL OFF!

Look for studs that can be used to join minifigures together.

WHAT A WORKOUT!

Use small LEGO® pieces to connect your minifigures.

Start with a base plate. The smaller the plate, the harder the challenge!

Likes Solving problems

Dislikes Boring hair colours

Weapon Duo-fusion blaster

=4-9=

Cyborg

The fierce-looking Cyborg was an ordinary human before she was upgraded with advanced technology. She now has fast reflexes and amazing computer abilities. The only thing she fears is running out of power!

WHAT IS A ROBOT'S FAVOURITE SNACK?

COMPUTER CHIPS.

Mega mech

Cyborg's friend Laser Mech is the coolest robotic hero in the universe. He even plays his own awesome theme tune.

Alien Trooper

The poor Alien Trooper has been asleep for many, many years. He has woken up and discovered that all of his advanced technology is completely out of date. He cannot conquer the galaxy now – but at least he had a good rest!

> WHY DID THE ALIEN GO TO THE DOCTOR?
>
> HE LOOKED A LITTLE GREEN!

Big name

This alien leads a huge interstellar empire. Her minions are not allowed to speak her name out loud (which is good, because it is very long and hard to say).

Mini Facts

Likes Taking over new worlds

Dislikes Alarm clocks

Weapon Laser blaster

Mini Facts

Likes Making spider decorations

Dislikes Websites crashing

Favourite accessory Her spider-silk cape

Spider Lady

Forget bats – this vampire loves spiders! Her castle is full of pet spiders and she makes her clothes from sticky spider silk. Spider Lady really likes the Fly Monster, but he avoids all her invitations to come over for a bite.

WHY DID THE VAMPIRE GO INTO THE CAVE?

TO HANG OUT!

Fly Monster

This creature was an ordinary fly until he was turned into a half-fly, half-minifigure hybrid. He is terrified of spiders!

Monster Scientist

The Monster Scientist is always experimenting and inventing new things, from rocket-propelled shoelaces to wacky monsters. He even experimented on his own brain to make it bigger ... but it just made him sillier than ever before!

> **WHAT DID THE SCIENTIST CALL HIS LATEST CREATION?**
>
> **A MONSTER-PIECE!**

Plant Monster

Monster Scientist gave his houseplant too much of an experimental plant food. It soon sprouted arms, legs and a monster appetite!

Mini Facts

Likes Being praised

Dislikes Safety warnings

Favourite creation Fly Monster

BUSY MINIFIGURES

Minifigures are an active bunch! They have busy jobs and lots of hobbies.

WATCH OUT! COMING THROUGH!

THERE'S A SPEED LIMIT YOU KNOW!

I'VE NEVER SEEN A CITY SHARK BEFORE ...

WOW! MY COSTUME MUST BE GOOD!

Astronaut

This daring guy has spent his whole life dreaming about going into space. He built toy spaceships and read every book about space he could find. He eats special space food, even when he is on Earth. Now, he is ready for blast off!

WHAT DO ASTRONAUTS EAT THEIR DINNER ON?

FLYING SAUCERS!

What if ... ?

Bang! The Scientist loves mixing things together and seeing what happens. Every experiment teaches her something new – even the ones that go wrong!

Likes Building LEGO® rockets

Dislikes Small meal pouches

Favourite subject Engineering

Mini Facts

Likes New places

Dislikes Cold hands

Favourite animal
Sloths – they are
good at staying still!

Wildlife Photographer

The adventurous Wildlife Photographer travels the world to get the perfect picture. She has been to hot savannahs to see lions and to chilly Antarctica to see penguins. She sets up her camera and waits ... and waits ... and waits. Click!

WHAT IS A RABBIT'S FAVOURITE TYPE OF MUSIC?

HIP HOP!

Helping hand

If an animal needs help, call the Vet. She will check a rabbit's hearing, give a giraffe a neck rub or even clean a crocodile's teeth!

Police Constable

The Police Constable is patrolling the streets. He watches out for trouble wherever he goes. He says a cheery hello to everyone he meets – unless they are committing a crime!

> WHAT DID THE POLICE OFFICER SAY TO HIS TUMMY?
>
> YOU ARE UNDER A VEST!

On the run

Look out, Constable! The Jewel Thief breaks into buildings to steal priceless gems. Unfortunately, she is also good at breaking out of jail!

Mini Facts

Likes Well-behaved people

Dislikes Dirty marks on his uniform

Favourite accessory Truncheon

CHALLENGE!

Guess who!

Choose a minifigure and see how quickly your friends can guess which one you have picked. They can only ask questions that can be answered with "yes" or "no"!

Take it in turns to choose a minifigure or ask the questions.

NO!

YES!

"IS YOUR MINIFIGURE DRESSED AS AN ANIMAL?"

Pick a character that might be hard to guess.

YES!

Hide your minifigure well out of sight!

33

Roller Derby Girl

This daring speedster never slows down – on or off the track. Her speed is useful when dashing and dodging around her rivals, but sometimes she cannot stop. She once found herself halfway across the world!

> WHY ARE MOUNTAINS SO FUNNY?
>
> THEY ARE HILL AREAS!

Happy hiker

The Hiker loves being outdoors. Nothing dampens his cheery mood, even getting lost in the middle of a rainstorm!

Mini Facts

Likes Winning a roller derby game

Dislikes Traffic jams

Best friend Race Car Guy – he shares her need for speed!

Mini Facts

Likes Doing tricks

Dislikes Dry land

Favourite animal
Sea turtle

Professional Surfer

This talented surfer has won every competition that he has entered. Now, he tests his surfing skills against the best athletes in the ocean – dolphins, manta rays and flying fish!

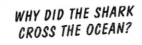

WHY DID THE SHARK CROSS THE OCEAN?

TO GET TO THE OTHER TIDE!

Fish out of water

This quirky guy used to be terrified of sharks, until he learned what amazing creatures they are. Now, sharks are his favourite animals!

Kickboxer

Kickboxing combines powerful punches and quick footwork, so the tough Kickboxer's feet are as quick as her fists! She once tried mixing up other sports, but no one wanted to play swim-tennis or go jog-bowling with her!

HOW DO YOU INVITE A WRESTLER TO A MATCH?

GIVE THEM A RING!

Loud and proud

The Wrestling Champion is very proud of his achievements and wants everyone to know it. Every time he wins a match, this show-off shouts about his victory!

Mini Facts

Likes Being active

Dislikes Tying shoelaces with her gloves on

Favourite colour Bright red

Minifigures love to party with their friends. It is time for a celebration!

KEEP ME AWAY FROM THOSE BALLOONS!

WHAT A BEAUTIFUL COSTUME!

DOES THIS PARTY HAVE SNACKS? I'M HUNGRY!

THIS IS THE BEST PARTY EVER!

Hot Dog Man

Everyone knows that Hot Dog Man loves hot dogs! He loves them so much that he has made his very own hot dog costume. His favourite type of party is a summer barbecue with – you've guessed it – lots of hot dogs!

WHY CAN'T THE MINIFIGURE RUN AWAY?

HIS FEET GET STUCK TO THE FLOOR!

Brick by brick

Brick Suit Guy likes to play speed building party games. Hopefully no one will think he is a real LEGO® brick and add him to their stack!

Mini Facts

Likes Hot dogs, of course!

Dislikes Spilling mustard

Favourite food Um ... hot dogs!

Mini Facts

Likes Giving gifts to her friends

Dislikes Balloons popping

Hobby Tying bows

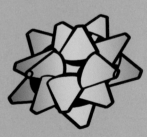

Birthday Party Girl

This little girl loves balloons, cake and party hats. When she finds the perfect gift for her friend, she opens and rewraps it again and again. She just gets so excited!

WHAT DID THE EGG SAY TO THE CLOWN?

YOU CRACK ME UP!

Clowning around

The wacky Party Clown can make any balloon animal that you could wish for ... as long as it is a dog!

Disco Diva

The Disco Diva is dressed to impress! She is always first onto the dance floor at parties. She likes to take control of the microphone, too. This superstar cannot help it – she was born to sing and dance!

WHY DID THE SINGER CLIMB A LADDER?

TO REACH THE HIGH NOTES!

Rock hard

Step aside, Disco Diva! The Rock Star is ready to perform his mega hit song "Brick Wall Baby". His fans are so excited!

Mini Facts

Likes Disco tunes

Dislikes The music being turned off

Favourite colour Purple

Mini Facts

Likes Surprises

Dislikes Cleaning his clothes

Favourite cake Chocolate

Cake Guy

Surpriiiiiise! Cake Guy has been waiting to surprise everyone by bursting out of a cake! There is icing everywhere, but luckily it is very tasty! Just how exactly did he fit into the cake?

WHY DID THE STUDENTS EAT THEIR HOMEWORK?

BECAUSE THEIR TEACHER SAID IT WAS A PIECE OF CAKE!

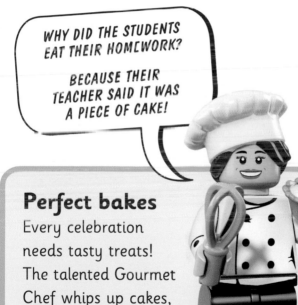

Perfect bakes

Every celebration needs tasty treats! The talented Gourmet Chef whips up cakes, pies and biscuits for all of her friends.

CHALLENGE!

Minifigure muddle

Mix up the heads, torsos and accessories of your minifigures. What is the most random character you can create?

Find minifigures with unusual costumes and accessories.

Cactus Girl

Cactus Girl thought her costume idea was fantastic, but now she keeps bumping into people and bursting balloons with her prickles. Her cactus arms also make it impossible to eat cake. Oops!

> WHAT DID THE FLOWER SAY TO THE CACTUS?
>
> YOU'RE LOOKING SHARP!

Beautiful bloom

Flowerpot Girl may seem shy, but she blossoms when she is having fun with Cactus Girl and her other cute friends.

Mini Facts

Likes Making costumes

Dislikes Ordinary clothes

Next costume idea Lobster (so she can pick things up!)

Mini Facts

Likes Winning prizes
Dislikes Slow coaches
Dream job Race car driver

Race Car Guy

3, 2, 1 … go! Competitive Race Car Guy always wants to be first in line for a slice of cake, first to open presents and to win every party game. He just really loves winning!

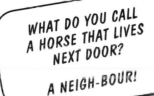

WHAT DO YOU CALL A HORSE THAT LIVES NEXT DOOR?

A NEIGH-BOUR!

Giddy up!
Is that a real horse? No, it is Cowboy Costume Guy and his clever party outfit! He loves telling silly jokes and horsing around.

Butterfly Girl

Happy Butterfly Girl loves bugs and hopes to get a job studying them one day. She shows her passion for insects with her pretty butterfly costume. She just wishes she could really fly!

HOW DO UNICORNS GET TO THE PARK?

ON A UNICYCLE!

Shiny happy unicorns

Unicorn Guy and Girl bring magic and adventure to everyone they meet. They also sprinkle glitter wherever they go!

Mini Facts

Likes All bugs
Dislikes Cold weather
Dream pet Caterpillar

Quiz

1. The Faun has legs like which animal?

2. Which minifigure has snakes instead of ordinary hair?

3. Which minifigure carries a duo-fusion blaster?

4. Who created the Plant Monster?

5. Where does the Wildlife Photographer travel to see penguins?

6. What is the Professional Surfer's favourite animal?

7. What colour kit does the Kickboxer wear?

8. What does Hot Dog Man dislike?

9. What is the name of the Rock Star's hit song?

10. Which minifigure would like to have a pet caterpillar?

BUILD A MINIFIGURE HOME

Why not make a minifigure display stand with LEGO®
bricks and plates? Build a simple structure that is stable
and balanced. Choose bright colours, or maybe use
a colour that matches your bedroom. It's up to you!

THERE'S ROOM FOR A LITTLE ONE!

Use colours that you have in your LEGO brick collection

Use plates with studs, not smooth tiles, so your minifigures can't fall off

NEW HEIGHTS
A height of five bricks is tall
enough to fit most minifigures
nicely. If your minifigure has a
large hat or helmet you may
need to make the level higher.

THE LEGO® IDEAS BOOK
YOU CAN BUILD ANYTHING!

OVER 500 IDEAS FROM LEGO FANS

Get inspired to build other
cool LEGO models!
Packed with more than
500 model ideas and top tips
for budding builders.

Underwater animals

Long, streamlined body

Bottlenose dolphin ▶

Dolphins can leap out the water high enough to jump over a double-decker bus! They communicate by making different clicking and whistling noises.

TRY BUILDING ME AND MY UNDERWATER FRIENDS!

◀ Blue-ringed octopus

This creature uses its tentacles to sense its surroundings. Watch out! It may look small and cute, but this species has deadly venom.

Learn more about amazing creatures from around the world. Build four animal models with the bricks inside, then see what else you can create!

Habitat facts

Australia's underwater Great Barrier Reef is so big, it can be **seen from space**. It's 2,000 km long and covers the same area as Italy!

Discover the awesome world of
THE LEGO® MOVIE 2™

Find out more!

Discover the name of Emmet's favourite plant (Planty), the secrets of the Systar System and more fun facts about THE LEGO® MOVIE 2™.

DID YOU KNOW?
Emmet has cream and 25 sugars in his coffee.

DID YOU KNOW?
One of Emmet's new friends is called Rex.

Have fun!

Relive the movie with more than **1,000** colourful stickers, including your favourite characters and cool new vehicles.

Explore!

Learn about Emmet, Lucy, Unikitty and the rest of the awesome heroes of THE LEGO MOVIE 2.

DID YOU KNOW?
When Unikitty gets angry she transforms into Ultrakatty!

Find out more at:
www.dk.com/LEGObooks

W ell **hello** there! We are

O verjoyed that you have **joined our celebration** of

R eading books and **sharing stories**, because we

L ove bringing **books** to you.

D id you know, we are a **charity** dedicated to celebrating the

B rilliance of **reading for pleasure** for everyone, everywhere?

O ur mission is to help you discover **brand new stories** and

O pen your mind to exciting **new worlds and characters**, from

K ings and queens to wizards and **pirates** to **animals** and **adventurers** and so many more. We couldn't

D o it without all the amazing **authors** and **illustrators**, booksellers and bookshops, publishers, schools and **libraries** out there –

A nd most importantly, we couldn't do it all without . . .

YOU!

On your bookmarks, get set, READ! Happy Reading. Happy World Book Day.

WORLD
**BOOK
DAY**

SHARE A STORY

From breakfast to bedtime, there's always time to discover and share stories together. You can . . .

1 TAKE A TRIP to your LOCAL BOOKSHOP

Brimming with brilliant books and helpful booksellers to share awesome reading recommendations, you can also enjoy booky events with your favourite authors and illustrators.

**FIND YOUR
LOCAL BOOKSHOP:**
booksellers.org.uk/
bookshopsearch

2 JOIN your LOCAL LIBRARY

That wonderful place where the hugest selection of books you could ever want to read awaits – and you can borrow them for FREE! Plus expert advice and fantastic free family reading events.

**FIND YOUR
LOCAL LIBRARY:**
gov.uk/local-library
-services/

3 CHECK OUT the **WORLD BOOK DAY** WEBSITE

Looking for reading tips, advice and inspiration? There is so much for you to discover at **worldbookday.com**, packed with fun activities, games, downloads, podcasts, videos, competitions and all the latest new books galore.

SPONSORED BY

**NATIONAL
BOOK
tokens**

Celebrate stories. Love reading.
World Book Day is a registered charity.